WHERE THERE IS LOVE

by

Jenny Claringbold

The extract from *The Clowns of God* by Maurice West is reproduced by permission of Hodder & Stoughton Ltd.

Where there is love

Copyright © Jenny Claringbold 1994

First published 1994 by Living Archive Press

Living Archive Press
The Old Bath House, 205 Stratford Road
Wolverton, Milton Keynes MK12 5RL

All rights reserved.
No part of this book may be reproduced, stored in a retrieval system, or transmitted in any form or by any means, electronic, mechanical, photocopying, recording or otherwise, without prior permission of the copyright holder or in accordance with the Copyright, Design and Patents Act 1988.

Cover design: Dylan Jeavons
Cover photograph: John Close

ISBN 0 904847 26 8

Acknowledgements

The transition from my initial manuscript to this book has needed many helping hands. Maggie and Roy Nevitt spent many hours editing my words, always believing they were worthy of publication. Roger Kitchen and his staff at the Living Archive Project were committed to getting it published.

This book has been made possible by a grant from the Abbey National Trust towards the work of the Living Archive Project in Milton Keynes. I hope that they approve of its use for this purpose.

David's paediatrician, G.P. and social worker took time out of their busy schedules to read the manuscript and offer constructive criticism and valuable advice.

Last, and by no means least, I want to acknowledge all my personal friends who supported and encouraged me to try to publish David's story. Over the years their friendship and love have meant so much not only to me but to all the family.

Jenny Claringbold

October 1994

Dedication

All that I have written I dedicate to David who is the endless rainbow in my life, and his brothers and sisters, who mean the world to me. Not forgetting John, my husband, who is very special to me and has been so patient and loving and allowed me to develop and grow.

Prologue

When my son, David, was six months old, he was diagnosed as suffering from a severe form of cerebral palsy. At the consultation with the professor who had examined David, we were advised that our son was affected in all four limbs, would be unable to walk or talk and be dependent on us as a baby for all his life, which wasn't expected to be beyond his early childhood, certainly not into adulthood. The doctor thought David could see, though he was unable to say to what extent, and he did have an acute sense of hearing. At least one good thing in his favour!

The news was absolutely devastating, as we had been looking forward to his arrival with such excitement. I had four children already from a previous marriage and this was to be my husband's first child. My pregnancy had been a difficult one, as I was affected by the Rhesus factor, which meant my baby had to have blood transfusions whilst in the womb and, because the problem was acute, I was actually in hospital for almost three months before the birth, which was carried out by Caesarean section.

David was taken to intensive care, as he was a poorly baby suffering from breathing problems and it was touch and go as to whether he would pull through. For several days his condition caused great anxiety but he eventually stabilised and improved and, at the age of two months, was able to come home to his family. We thought then that all our worries were over but they had only just begun.

I tried desperately to care for him but he was constantly crying and fretful, so we returned to the hospital for advice. It was after several weeks of routine tests that we were told our son had brain damage.

In my heart, I had been expecting the worst but was determined to bring out the best in David and prove the doctors wrong.

The professor had told us the worst and said any little improvement on that would be a bonus. Well, during David's life, we've had many heartaches and tears but there have been many bonuses too.

His cheerfulness and contentment have brought him through serious orthopaedic operations and subsequent severe chest infections which have increased to the degree that he is rarely 100% well and often close to death.

At present there is a great deal of debate going on as to whether children born in similar circumstances to David should be allowed to die at birth, rather than hospitals spend so much of their scarce financial resources resuscitating these babies that perhaps will not be able to contribute to society in later life. Certainly I would agree that caring for someone like my son is physically and emotionally draining but I think I speak for all his family when I say that knowing David has made us evaluate life and know the true meaning of love and happiness.

What I would say is that, as parents of a severely handicapped child, we would have preferred in the early days to be credited with a degree of common sense and to be given all the facts before decisions were made on our child's health care programme, rather than find out at a later date there could have been alternative choices. This aspect of his care was often difficult but over the years I have learned to have confidence in myself as David's carer and mother and have tactfully requested what I know is best for my son.

Apart from short spaces of time when David has respite care, I devote twenty four hours a day to his needs, so feel this counts for something. I am very fortunate now to have a medical team caring for my son that understands my feelings too and I value this. However, I realise that, in trying to achieve this goal, I have often proved myself to be a difficult parent.

David has proved all the doctors wrong by growing into a happy, smiling and intelligent young man who just loves life, despite the frailty of his body. Because of his determination to enjoy his life whatever, I thought our experiences should be put down and recorded in a little book to be lost in the attic and brought out several years after. He's too precious to forget and has brought much joy and happiness to our family. Later, it was suggested by a friend that I should try to have this book published as it could prove to be of some comfort and hopefully inspire parents and families in a similar situation. I hope so.

Some months ago, I read a book called 'The Clowns of God' by Maurice West, which deals with the second coming of Jesus Christ. To make His presence known, the man who calls himself 'Jesus' sits a young Downs' syndrome girl by him and, in comforting her, speaks these most profound words to unbelieving adults around him:-

'I know what you are thinking. You need a sign. What better one could I give than to make this little one whole and new? I could do it but I will not. I am the Lord, not a conjurer. I gave this mite a gift I denied to all of you - eternal innocence. To you she looks imperfect but to me she is flawless, like the bud that dies unopened or the fledgling that falls from the nest to be devoured by the ants.

'She will never offend me, as all of you have done. She will never pervert or destroy the work of my father's hands. She is necessary to you. She will evoke the kindness that will keep you human. Her infirmity will prompt you to gratitude for your own good fortune. More. She will remind you every day that I am who I am, that my ways are not yours, and that the smallest dust mite whirled in darkest space does not fall out of my hand. I have chosen you. You have not chosen me. This little one is a sign to you. Treasure her!'

In a strange way I believe that David's life, as it has turned out, was meant to be, and it has certainly been an experience, not just for me but for everyone that knows him and has shared his life.

As I say in my little book: where there is love, nothing is impossible. We certainly love and treasure David.

A Difficult Pregnancy

Where to begin? Perhaps from the beginning might be best.

I was born on 4th October 1946, my father's birthday and my parents' wedding anniversary. I was the fifth of six children, having three brothers and two sisters, and home was always a very lively and happy place to be.

My mother's life was far from easy, raising children through the war years single-handed, as my father served abroad with the army. Even after the war, he continued to work unsociable hours with his responsible job as head chef of large hotels.

Mother ran the house in a very orderly fashion; the place was spotlessly clean but homely and, as we children grew up, we were expected to help out where we could with shopping and odd jobs.

We respected our parents and their word was law. None of us rebelled, as you hear teenagers doing today and we have each gone on to do as best we can and make the most of our lives.

When my youngest brother was just three years old, my father, then in his early fifties, suffered a stroke and life as we knew it was never the same again. For a man who had never had a day's illness in his life, it was very sad to see. He became quite dependent on our mother, not having full use of his limbs and unable to care properly for himself. His memory and speech were also permanently impaired, which was really sad, for my young brother did not have the opportunity to hold long conversations with him and learn from his wisdom, as we had been able to do.

Nevertheless, Dad never gave up willingly and I believe we all learned to cope with adversity through seeing his strength of courage.

From very early on in life, I wanted to become a nurse. I was no great academic and I hoped I could succeed in my ambition. I applied for a pre-nursing course at one of our local hospitals and was accepted, much to my pleasure, so started work on leaving school in 1963.

We worked for three months in each department other than the wards, which gave us an insight into hospital procedures and, for my final time before starting training proper, I was allowed to work on the children's ward. It was here that I truly learned to understand the responsibilities of nursing. There were many sick and poorly children, all needing lots of love and cuddles when their parents weren't around. In those days, visiting times were very strict.

I really felt this was where my future lay and I was prepared to work hard to achieve my ambition.

Therefore, I was certainly quite unprepared for the emotions that overcame me when I met Max, who was working at the hospital during the college recess. His face was generally the first I would see as I came to work each morning. He was very good-looking, with a warm and friendly smile and I suppose it was love at first sight, as they say.

When I went to work at the hospital, I felt that being a nurse would be my vocation and I hadn't really considered the fact that I might meet someone whom I'd want to marry. I'd had other boyfriends, some serious, but marriage was never even a consideration. However, with Max, things developed to the point where I felt I had to make a choice. It wasn't really difficult to realise I wanted to be his wife and, hopefully, a mother and I believe in giving up my career I made the right choice. I took alternative work in an office and we married at a local registrar's office on 25th November 1967.

We had four children, the eldest, a daughter, Jayne; followed by three sons, Nicholas, James and Charles. I have Rhesus negative blood and Max was Rhesus positive. The two blood types being incompatible, I produced antibodies as the pregnancies progressed. Jayne had been born healthy at hospital but Nicholas, our second child, born at home, was slightly jaundiced. James, born in hospital, needed an exchange of blood when he was two days old. Wanting a second daughter, I fell pregnant quickly after James's birth.

We had never had any genetic counselling. No-one had ever advised us of the dangers of my pregnancies, so, because we were young, in love and wanted a family of four, all close in age, we just went ahead. I had come from a large family myself and felt I could cope quite happily with the little brood, our idea being that, by the time they were all teenagers, we would still be young enough to enjoy our life together.

It wasn't until our fourth child was expected that I heard from the medical staff at the hospital that, with my blood, there were risks attached to my quick succession of pregnancies. My own GP said that, although I had a large number of antibodies already in my blood, no complications would occur until at least the sixth month of pregnancy, at which stage I would be passed over to my local maternity hospital. This is what happened, so you can imagine how surprised I was to be whisked into hospital at that time. I felt very confused, as I was still unaware of the seriousness of the situation. To make matters worse, I could not go into my own local hospital but had to be transferred to a hospital in southeast London which was equipped to deal with my problems.

A series of amniocentesis tests showed my unborn child was severely anaemic and it was possible that I could lose the baby. I was given two inter-uterine transfusions that week to counteract the anaemia and further tests to confirm they had been successful. It was after the second amniocentesis test was done that Charles was born. I was very well cared for and kept informed of his frail condition. Despite the fact that he was born at 35 weeks, his weight was reasonable and his lungs matured sufficiently to help him through.

Over the next forty-eight hours, four exchange transfusions were given and he slowly progressed. After six days, I was allowed home but Charles needed to stay in the special care unit for two months until he was strong and healthy. On leaving hospital, he had a few set-backs, after which he began to thrive and has never looked back since. He grew into a strong little lad, happy and full of spirit. My father passed away in June 1971, whilst I was expecting our fourth child, so it seemed fitting to name Charles after his grandfather, who had fought equally hard to live for twelve years following his initial illness.

On leaving hospital, I was advised not to have any more children for at least six years, which would give the antibodies a chance to subside. Better still, I was advised to consider a sterilisation. This, at 24, seemed a drastic step and one which, later, I was pleased not to have taken.

Sadly, my marriage didn't last. I still loved my husband dearly but by mutual agreement we parted and I spent two years bringing up the children alone. We were divorced in 1972.

I can look back and smile now at my first marriage and the eventful lives of my children. Life was often difficult but rarely dull. Jayne was always big sister to her brothers. She was just walking when Nicholas was born and, by the time James arrived, she was able to help dress her brother and help with the baby, fetching and carrying and probably getting in the way often as well. When Charles was born, she really had become the perfect little mother to them all. Nevertheless, when she chose, she could also be the perfect little madam as well as tomboy, climbing trees and playing football alongside her brothers!

The divorce was not easy for Max or me to cope with but the children were able to manage the situation better. I tried as best I could to allow their Dad to come and go freely. Even so, it was still upsetting for everyone at times; lots of tears and confusion. Max was the eternal child, the one they could easily respond to without guilt or question, for they were all so much in his likeness, sharing his humour and wit. I was just content to be at home with them, sharing all those special moments of childhood, with lots of time to myself to reflect and often regret.

Close friends took me out occasionally and were there to keep me company in my lonely moments. When Jayne and Nicholas were both at school and the younger boys had settled into play-group, I was able to take a part-time job in a local shop. It was this step that was to change my life and those of my children.

A single man managed the shop and we worked very well together. John was a very caring man and in time got to know my circumstances. Wanting to cheer my life a little, he invited me to a Henry Mancini concert at the Royal Albert Hall one evening in May 1974. It was a wonderful evening; at the end of it, we both felt comfortable in each other's company. Next day he asked me out again and things progressed from there. He seemed to accept me just as I was and asked nothing of me but my company. To have someone who really cared, was a wonderful feeling.

He also accepted my children, which for a man who had had little contact with young children, was good to see. Our relationship developed into something quite special and even though we hadn't known each other very long, we discussed marriage and the future. Just five months after that first date, we were married on 24th October, 1974.

A couple of weeks before the wedding, I realised I was pregnant and worried for John. I asked what he thought I should do for the best. He was adamant. He wanted the child but was concerned for me, realising my past history.

We quickly sought medical advice and were told it would be reasonably safe to continue with the pregnancy. Termination was also discussed - not that I thought lightly on this subject - but it had to be faced as an alternative. John wanted his child; I wanted his child; our minds were made up to face the difficulties I might encounter.

It would be necessary, we were told, to have regular amniocentesis tests and be ready to be admitted for treatment from about the fourth month.

My husband's family were a tower of strength during the next few months caring not only for John but our four little children as well. By the beginning of February 1975, I was advised an inter-uterine transfusion was necessary and we arranged for the family to be cared for as I packed my bags ready for admission. The ward at the hospital was familiar, as were the senior staff and procedures but the length of admission was longer than I bargained for.

At the first instance, I was admitted for 10 days but eventually I spent the best part of 14 weeks within those same four walls. It was thought safer for me to stay put rather than go home and risk a miscarriage, much to my annoyance and disappointment.

There we were, newly married; John, who'd only known the children a short while, coping with all eventualities; and me, trapped in hospital for what seemed like an eternity. The days seemed long, the nights even worse and the waiting I wouldn't envy any mother now. It was only my desire to keep this baby, my husband's child, that kept me sane.

On bad days, when my spirits were low, everywhere I tried to escape to was the same. I was faced with more windows and walls and, in the corridors, happy parents, leaving with their new-born babies. During my stay in hospital, I had to have four inter-uterine transfusions to help save my child. It was, at that time, a very dangerous procedure and there were many miscarriages and premature labours occurring weekly on the ward. We, as patients, felt for every one of our mothers and there was a great comradeship amongst us whilst we idled the long days away.

As I went to sleep each night, I prayed for my husband and my young family whom I longed to see each weekend when they were able to visit but hated having to say goodbye to after their brief visits. It was lovely to get their little notes and pictures, all of which I have kept still, and the sound of their little voices on the telephone each evening brought an ache to my heart. I would spend the next hour or so weeping uncontrollably in my only refuge - the bathroom. I think each mother suffered the same after their visits.

We must have been the cleanest pregnant mums in S.E. London but must have run up the water-rate bill for the NHS in the process!

After the fourth successful transfusion, I continued to have weekly amnio tests to determine the maturity of my baby's lungs. I have since learned that these tests alone are quite dangerous and carry their own risks to pregnancy. I don't believe I am alone in saying that one is somewhat unaware of the dangers and risks involved at these times. One accepts a situation in the hope that it is for the baby's good and many mothers are not equipped to ask searching questions. Equally, patients are not always offered the information we would like to hear. Nowadays, perhaps because of media coverage of medical matters, things may be different. I certainly hope so.

Life works in strange ways sometimes. It felt like I had been in the hospital for months, not just six weeks, and despite the friendships that were made between mums, there were times I felt desperately lonely. The arrival of a new expectant mum was to change all that.

Pauline was admitted to our ward for bedrest for the final few weeks of her pregnancy. Her husband had brought her into hospital and settled her in the bed that was directly opposite mine. When he finally left, she was naturally feeling very low, so I went across to introduce myself and cheer her up.

Pauline had a lovely face, open, warm and friendly and she was what I like to describe as 'a big lady'. This extra weight, alongside suffering from asthma, as well as being heavily pregnant, meant she had been going through a bad time. She was quite rightly concerned about having to stay in hospital, having not been long married herself, and we spent many hours consoling each other and keeping spirits high. She was great fun to be with, and we often sat talking long after 'lights-out', completing the crossword and drinking tea, before reluctantly obeying Sister's advice to get a little sleep. She gave me support when I needed it and our unique friendship seemed sealed forever. I think this friend was heaven-sent!

One Sunday, about four weeks after her admission to the ward, our lunch was interrupted by Pauline being whisked away to deliver a healthy little son. After so many weeks of waiting, we were just so thankful that everything eventually turned out well for her.

Then, after what seemed an eternity waiting, one Friday morning I was told by my doctor I would be induced on the Monday. Wonderful news; at long last, the waiting was over and now it was my turn to be given tea and toast at 5 a.m. and sent off to the labour ward, with the encouraging words and smiles from my fellow patients.

Enter David

John had arranged to be with me during labour. Shy though he was, he had prepared himself for helping me and seeing his child born. Within an hour, I was attached to a drip to assist the procedure and John's smile and comforting word kept my spirits up.

At three in the afternoon, things didn't seem to be progressing and, by early evening, I still hadn't produced. I was taken off the drip and sent to the X-ray Department where it was discovered that the baby was lying in a very difficult position. I would not be able to have a natural childbirth. Caesarean section was rapidly arranged and at 10.30 p.m. on Monday 28th April 1975, our son, David Jonathan, made his first appearance in this big wide world.

My husband caught a fleeting glance of this little scrap being rushed to the special care unit in a mobile oxygen tent. I knew little of the next few hours and can vaguely remember being told at 4 a.m. the following morning that I had a son. My first thoughts were that my daughter would be disappointed. She was hoping for a little sister and no doubt would be upset that Helen was in fact David.

For the next three days, I was confined to bed feeling very low; no doubt the operation had taken its toll after such a long stay in hospital. My body was obviously weak and unprepared for the ordeal I had just experienced. On reflection I did not give too much thought to my new son in those first few hours. What I did feel was a detachment. It had been a long wait for him to arrive and having looked forward to a natural childbirth, the Caesarean section had severed any strong feelings I had for this new little boy in my life.

It wasn't that I didn't worry about him. I felt quite desperate to see him but, the longer I was kept away, the worse those feelings of detachment became. It was like hearing reports of someone else's child. "He's fine", they'd say, "he's doing O.K."

It all meant very little, partly because I had been quite ill following the birth. I had developed some kind of infection in my womb and was running a high temperature. But, after two days, I became quite anxious to see this little baby everyone kept calling my son.

The morning after the birth a paediatrician had visited me with her apologies that David had been induced too soon. "They should have waited another week, then the lungs would have been able to cope. Another week would have made all the difference."

"What do you intend to call him?" she asked, having already drawn the curtains around my bed. "David Jonathan", I replied, feeling numbed with shock. "I'm so sorry", was all she could say, as she left me weeping quietly. How unfair, was all I could think. She's told me on my own, without my husband here with me, that David is fighting for his life. I need my husband here. Pauline heard my tears and came in at that time to comfort me. Together we cried and eventually I tried to pull myself together. I felt wretched.

John arrived back to see me later that day and it was decided that, as soon as I was fit, I could go up to visit David in the special care unit. Also holding me back was the fact that the lift had broken down and I wasn't strong enough to climb several flights of stairs. They would not allow David off the unit so all I could do was wait.

John had been up to see David twice a day since he was born and excitedly on the fourth day we went up to see our son together for the first time. David looked so tiny lying in the oxygen tent. He was as well as could be expected, they advised, and seeing his tiny frame struggling for life, I held my breath and wondered if he would pull through at all. We left the unit in silence. We couldn't stay long, partly because I wasn't feeling strong enough and partly because we felt so inadequate. There was little we could do but to wait and pray he would survive.

I was eventually well enough to leave hospital after twelve days but David was to stay another six weeks, during which time he slowly gained weight and became stronger and healthier. When David eventually came home to us, I had recovered pretty much from my long stay in hospital and felt able to cope with my new son.

A Poor Start

It seemed very strange at first having David home. We had to get to know him all over again and it was so difficult, because, unlike all my other children, he couldn't suck properly from the bottle and spent so long crying. He took ages to feed because of this and no sooner had he fallen asleep following a feed than he was awake again crying. I couldn't comfort him and neither could John.

Normally, if a baby is fretful, a cuddle from either Mum or Dad works wonders to calm it. Just the knowing instinct that the comfort and body smell is familiar is usually enough to quell the tears and bring peace and contentment. But no, David just went on crying continually, a high-pitched unusual cry, when his whole body would tighten up and his little fists were clenched as in a rage.

And so it went on for the next few weeks. I tried sleeping when David slept, snatching a few minutes peace here and there and, when he woke again screaming, I tried desperately to satisfy him. My husband worked long days, so it seemed unfair to ask him to be up in the night. Thankfully, by this time, only Charles was at home during the day, so I could catch up with the odd forty winks, providing David settled for a short while.

Somehow we never seemed to reach David; everyone tried, but he seemed to sleep little and cry far too often. He was very tiny, because of his weight loss after birth. I tried to change his feeding habits and attempted mixed feeding with no success. Eventually, I took him to see our own G.P. It wasn't the first time I'd spoken to him about David, but this time his approach was different. He opened his tiny clenched fists to examine his palms, then he looked at me and quietly said, "I think you'd best take David to see the paediatrician at the hospital where he was born".

Deep down inside, I had always thought something was wrong with David. Even before he was born, during my long stay in hospital, it all seemed so unreal, so mechanical. That the foetus growing inside of me was some sort of machine; that at any stage it could be damaged. All the treatment was given so methodically, cold and calculating. I was a number, that was all, a pregnant woman with a number.

Even when the gynaecologist visited each Monday morning, she would start on the opposite side of the ward to me at bed no.1, talking to the mothers, examining and questioning and would continue in this fashion throughout until she came to me. Then, standing at the foot of the bed, she would read my notes, glance up and ask "Baby moving, mother?" "Yes," I would say, and without further ado she would give a half-hearted smile and disappear out of the ward. She had done that every Monday regularly since I had been admitted. It was like being conditioned into this state, to prepare me for the worst. I had four babies who'd done all the usual things but, somehow even making allowances for David's poor start in life, things didn't really add up.

We went along to see the paediatrician next morning without delay, clutching a letter from our own doctor. She gave David a thorough examination and advised me I had done wrong to change his milk. It was indigestible to him and that was the reason for his fretfulness. She then went on to say that because all my other children had been contented, easy-to-manage babies, now that I had one that was fretful, I couldn't cope!

We were sitting in a very small office, and I can distinctly recall sitting on my hands, for as she told me this, my instinct was to want to strangle her for such a statement! Not that I am a violent person at all; I was just so horrified and outraged at her assumption. If I thought that David's fretfulness was purely attention-seeking, I would never have been there in the first place. I tried to tell her this in the politest way I could. I had tried for two months to satisfy this little baby who had cried and screamed almost every hour of every day. I had attempted everything possible to satisfy him, including cuddling him constantly and sleeping with him in our bed, as well as leaving him alone to cry it out. Nothing worked; he just became more tearful and more tense. That was the reason I had gone to see the doctor, because I felt something else was wrong with him.

Reluctantly she said she would admit him for routine observations.

A Flicker Of Hope

Two weeks passed without any conclusions being drawn, other than a nurse saying to us his cry sounded 'abnormal' whatever that meant. Then some days later, we were advised that a brain scan was to be carried out. Before those results were given to us, we were interviewed by a social worker at the hospital as to our circumstances at home. This included such questions as to whether we had gas or electric central heating, carpet on the floors and curtains at the windows. The social worker also enquired how my children had accepted David and how my new husband regarded his step-children.

Being somewhat naive and also extremely concerned about David, the penny didn't drop until she asked the final question and added "Just in case David is allowed home again with you". Had she thought we were child abusers? We'll never know but I never want to experience such an intimidating interview again.

A few days later we received a telephone call to visit the hospital at 7 p.m. that evening. We arrived on the children's ward to be greeted in the corridor by a Casualty Officer, who had been asked to convey the results of the tests on behalf of the paediatrician, who was otherwise engaged. We were told, standing as we were in the corridor, that the results were positive; our son was brain-damaged. He could tell us no more other than it was best if we took David home. He was leaning up against a post as he spoke, like he was explaining tomorrow's weather forecast. He wasn't English and his lack of communication was appalling at such a dreadful time.

"I can't discuss the case further", he said. "I don't even know the child. You will be given a letter to visit an expert in these matters at one of the London teaching hospitals. Goodnight."

And with that he was gone, leaving us standing, devastated by such news.

I had been half expecting these results (mother's intuition, I suppose) but for John poor John, a bombshell had just been dropped and the bottom had fallen out of his life. The journey home seemed even longer than usual, the doctor's words going round and round in our heads. From somewhere, we gathered the strength to phone the news to our parents and then explain in simple terms to the children, then aged 7, 6, 5 and 4, that David was a poorly baby.

Fortunately, the appointment to see the Professor followed within a couple of days and what set out to be a cold resume of our future life with David was in fact a very heart-warming experience. Now just five months old, the doctor we saw put our son through his paces. He started at his head and working down his tiny body to his toes, he left no nerve-ending unchecked.

First the Professor confirmed that, yes, David was handicapped by Cerebral Palsy, which meant that he was spastic in all four limbs, and he was also brain-damaged, probably staying as a baby for the whole of his life, which we were told was unforeseeable, but not to expect him to live into adulthood. He was also unable to sit unaided, had very bad head control and, as he appeared to look constantly at the ceiling, his eyesight had also been affected but the doctor was unsure to what degree. The eyes were perfectly formed; it was the nerves going from the eye to the brain that were affected.

David probably would never speak. Fortunately, his hearing was acute, at least one small thing in his favour, but sadly, said the doctor, the future held little in the way of improvement; in fact life with David was going to be pretty bleak.

"We have to tell you this," he explained, "then any little improvement is certainly going to be a bonus."

He prescribed a low dose of Diazepam which would help relax David so that the spasms and stiffness would ease and hopefully make David more content and easier to handle. He also advised physiotherapy and all available assistance was offered, especially moral support from those trained to help.

After all, caring for David was now going to be an ongoing situation, possibly for all his life, as he would never become independent as our other children would be.

It seemed all too much to take in at the time. John looked at me and I at him, as David was handed back into my arms. I can remember thinking to myself, "Don't cry now, be strong." I knew if I let go it would certainly upset John, who was, by now, looking extremely shocked and pale. How could all this be possible? Wasn't David such a beautiful baby, bright eyed, fair-skinned, blonde hair and so normal looking!

The diagnosis seemed incredible, so difficult to comprehend. John reached out and took his little hand, somehow trying to keep in his emotions. We were feeling desperately low at this point, really just wanting to get away from the hospital and share in each other's grief. We loved one another so deeply, had sacrificed so much time in our early marriage during my long stay in hospital and, now, what was supposed to be a happy future with our new son was so bleak and full of unknown fears.

From seeing the Professor, we were taken directly into the physiotherapy room, where we were introduced to the head of department. We were greeted with a smile and cheery word from the tall bespectacled man who scooped David from my arms and threw him into the air, catching him gently in his sturdy arms.

"Hello, you fine little man", he said, "You're a great little fellow, aren't you?"

He sat him on his lap, talking straight to David, glancing reassuringly at John and me. Suddenly, the cloud that had descended on me in the previous room lifted. Perhaps things wouldn't be quite so terrible after all. David was alive and he could see a little and hear well and, yes, we'd just been told he was severely handicapped but he was our son. We loved him before the diagnosis; still do, no matter what. That would never falter. I thought then, as I do now, Where there is love, nothing is impossible. Our life would be more difficult, for sure, but somehow I felt a deeper strength, as though someone was helping me face the future, right from this very moment.

The meeting was brief. The physiotherapist advised us that exercises would help develop David's abilities and he asked that we bring him along on a weekly basis to learn these with help from the staff, so that we could carry out the treatment at home.

With this in mind, it was hoped that David might be able to develop such skills as to hold his own head squarely on his shoulders and perhaps use his arms and legs. This would obviously not happen overnight, if at all. It might take months, even years to develop just one of these skills but I for one was willing to give it a try. So we said our goodbyes to this Bringer of Hope and set off for home.

Our journey home was a quiet one, the doctor's words going round and round in our head and the vivid picture of David with the physiotherapist somehow being a flicker of hope in the gloom.

Once home, explaining to parents the events of the day was a difficult task. John's mother, a widow, had been looking forward to seeing her little grandson growing up and doing all the things that would bring back cherished memories of her own son's childhood. Now, for her as well, it was difficult to visualise what the future might hold.

We also tried to explain to our own little family that their baby brother was a very special child, loved by us all but somehow always to be different from them, perhaps never being able to achieve as much as they would.

Except for my own family, who were devastated by the news and still find difficulty in accepting David and all his problems, my overall fears for David's acceptance were unfounded as he came to be loved by everyone. He had such an appealing little face which would lighten up at the various greetings from friends and relatives. Through everyone's kind support, the first few months were made easier for both John and me.

With constant physiotherapy we managed to teach David to grasp a small toy in his right hand. It was a wooden cube with a bell inside, which made it all the more interesting for him. Because of the strong spasm, he would drop the toy just seconds after gripping it but, never mind, it was still the beginning of an achievement and we were so pleased with his efforts.

Despite the help of the relaxing medication, he was still quite a fretful little boy and so at times we resorted to using a dummy. Yes, the dreaded dummy, but this time it actually helped in more ways than one. We would not only achieve the peace most parents expect when a child sucks on the dummy but it would at the same time teach David where his face was.

This probably sounds ridiculous but unless David was helped to touch areas of his body, he appeared totally unaware of its existence. By giving him a dummy in the one hand he could use, he would take his hand up to his forehead, guide the hand down his nose and then find his mouth. Simple really, but so wonderful.

Why Me?

Why me? This was the question that kept going round in my mind when David was about a year old. Things had gone relatively smoothly for a few months and we were all adapting to our new way of life and its limitations. A life I hadn't really expected, but one which had been plotted out for us, I believe, and we, as a family, had to make the best of it.

I can remember a time, when alone, I began to feel so upset, so resentful, that all these things were happening to us. We hadn't asked for it all to happen; we hadn't wished for it to happen but it was all going on now. It seemed at that moment in time to be a tragedy, a terrible, terrible, tragedy. I asked myself over and over again, why it had to happen to us - ME? Surely, after so many weeks spent in hospital, the medical staff should have realised there was a problem, that our baby was at risk. And why wasn't I given a Caesarean section as a matter of course, then perhaps he would have been born healthy instead of handicapped.

All these questions kept going round in my head and I felt unable to talk to anyone, least of all my husband. For one thing, I didn't want to upset him and for another no-one could begin to understand the anger and deep frustration I was feeling. We were trying so hard to care for David, trying to treat him as a normal child but with a handicap, inside I felt it was a big battle and I was losing. In the end, I just broke down and cried and cried.

It happened one day at a physiotherapy session, not intentionally, but really it was the best thing that could have happened. One of the doctors helping with David's treatment was on hand and took me into a side-room, telling me not to be afraid of my emotions. It was quite normal and, after all, for almost a year we had coped so well, it was perhaps inevitable that I should reach breaking point sooner or later. I just continued to weep buckets. All those inner fears and anxieties I had held on to came rushing out in a torrent.

The doctor explained that unless I voiced my feelings, problems, fears, hard though it might be, the medical staff would not be able to help us. On the face of it, I had appeared to be managing very nicely but underneath my thin layer of confidence, there was a volcano erupting. When it did, everything and everybody got burned. We continued to talk for near on an hour, until I felt calmer and then he suggested that David might be best admitted to the children's ward for a few days to enable me to have a rest.

Reluctantly, I agreed and the first time of parting with David was so painful, yet inside I knew I needed to give him over to the hospital to allow me to have a break.

Caring for David almost 24 hours a day, however much we loved him, was a strenuous task, not just physically but more especially emotionally. Added to that, we had the other children to consider, for we didn't want them to suffer unnecessarily either.

During that week, although I still visited David each day, I was able to have a good rest and reassess the situation. I also had the opportunity and the confidence to talk everything through with my husband. Life had been very hectic over the past two years and I hadn't really given myself the chance to come to terms with all the events. I thought I was strong enough to cope one hundred per cent on my own.

Although I had managed in the past when my marriage folded and I was left to bring up my four children; I could see no reason why I couldn't manage on my own now. I really thought I didn't need outside help and, besides, other people didn't understand. How wrong I was. People around me were only too aware of my inner sadness, grief and unhappiness, all those feelings I had tried to hide. I wanted to be seen to be coping and I had to come to terms with the fact that I needed those people to help too in our new life with David.

I wanted to enjoy my time with David in the family and with everyone's help I began to think in a positive way again. David's progress was extremely slow in every way. He was unable to sit unaided and couldn't control his head, so it would flop backwards onto his shoulders.

David was very stiff limbed which meant play was limited and toilet training couldn't even be considered for a long while yet. Still he was such a happy child and it gave me heart to continue when I would get smiles and laughter in response; nothing else seemed to matter. The handicaps became secondary whilst David was so responsive.

As time went by, we came to realise we couldn't live in the same house with our large family growing up around us and all David's equipment to care for him; we desperately needed more space. At the same time, John had become disillusioned with his work, so we came to the decision that we would apply to move out of London and start a new life in an expanding new town in Buckinghamshire.

The move was to be a very complicated procedure, especially having David to consider. There were endless forms to fill in and questions to answer as to what care our son would require and whether the area we wanted to move to could provide for his needs, as well as considering the older children.

Thankfully, we were accepted and were given a moving date but, unfortunately for David, about four months before we moved from London, he was taken ill one morning and suffered a long epileptic fit. It was a very disturbing experience, taking David to hospital where he was treated and kept in the ward for a couple of days for observation.

On David's discharge, we were advised that another fit could occur at any time and then he would need to be prescribed medication to control the situation. I tried to put this set-back to one side and concentrate on planning our move, hoping it was just a one-off occurrence which can happen with young babies for no apparent reason.

We had talked through our decision to make a fresh start coming to the conclusion that London didn't hold a lot for us now and we wanted the best for our growing family. Everything seemed to point to a better life for us all so, in February 1978, we left our familiar surroundings for a new venture in life and one which we have never regretted.

On returning occasionally to visit relatives, our roots are still there and often it will pull at the heartstrings but, once we return to our home here, we realise this is where we belong. Having no relatives nearby meant we had to cope completely alone but happily it has made us all better people for our new-found independence.

As for David's care, we have never looked back; everyone has been so helpful. No sooner were we in our new home than we were advised by the Education Authorities that David could perhaps attend school on a part-time basis. For this purpose, he had to be fully assessed and was then allocated a place at a suitable unit twice a week for a couple of hours, which gave me a little free time to just sit and relax or do chores that couldn't be done when David was around.

Coping with a large family including a handicapped child, I had to get the housework down to a fine art, whereby everything was done to make life easier. A quick clean through the house every day meant I stayed on top of the dust and, when buying clothes, nothing was purchased unless it was machine-washable, requiring as little ironing as possible.

It was enjoyable watching the family settling into their new surroundings, making new friends and having far more space to enjoy themselves than we had been used to back in London. However, we still valued our friendships with those people we had left behind.

Our friendship with Pauline, whom I'd met in hospital whilst expecting David, had developed into a unique relationship. We had become very close, like sisters, so even though we lived a distance from one another, we spoke regularly on the telephone and visited each other as often as possible, offering help and support. She and her husband were such happy people and so caring they meant a great deal to us. Therefore, when her second son was born soon after we moved here, we were delighted to be asked to be his godparents. Friendships like that don't happen often and we treasured ours.

We had not long moved into our new house when David was taken ill again. This time, at night. I called the doctor and he came out immediately to administer medication to stop the fit, which had lasted almost an hour. Later, he was prescribed phenobarbitone which apparently can either help to calm the patient or have the opposite effect. With David it chose to take the negative response, so, for the next week, he was extremely fretful and spent most of his waking hours just screaming and crying.

Once the medical staff had decided for themselves it was not helpful for David, the drug was stopped and a more suitable one prescribed. David calmed down and peace came to the household again. Then a few weeks later, again in the dead of night, I was woken by David having yet another epileptic fit. Within minutes of phoning the doctor, he had arrived, together with an ambulance and before I knew it, I was speeding up the motorway to our nearest casualty unit. We arrived in a little under fifteen minutes; for a journey of some twenty three miles, that's some going.

On our arrival, David was met by the casualty staff, who did everything they could to pull him through, as by now the fit had lasted well into a hour and his breathing was failing fast. I can remember praying with all my might that he should be given another chance and to my utter relief his breathing began to stabilise. He was transferred to the children's ward and I sat with him through the night, whilst he lay in a deep sleep.

The following day an E.E.G. was carried out to check for brain damage but the doctors said it was very difficult to assess, because obviously he already had a certain amount with the cerebral palsy. We could only hope that he would continue to progress despite this setback. After almost a week in hospital with David, stabilised, on increased medication, I was able to take him home again and he returned to school.

Even with these setbacks, David began to make up for his poor start in life and became very responsive and happy despite his weak little body. At five years of age he was quite tall, although his limbs were wasted through lack of exercise. We were able to get certain sounds from him in response to our questions. If asked if he was thirsty and wanted a drink, he would give an 'mmm' sound and stick out his tongue to show he wanted a drink. He loved to hear nursery rhymes especially 'this little piggy' and 'round and round the garden'. He began to know them so well; he would laugh even before I got to the line where he would be tickled.

These abilities were always a source of amusement to visitors, who, seeing this little boy sitting quietly in his chair, didn't realise his sense of humour when played with in such a way. He certainly had a wicked sense of humour and could always see the funny side to a sad situation. One was never allowed to be upset with David around. If you knocked yourself and began hopping around the room in pain, David would think that hilarious. If you accidently dropped something (say a cup) or made a foolish mistake with your work, he would shriek with laughter, so home was always a happy one.

A Few Steps Forward

David always had a session of physiotherapy at school each week and I would go along to see what treatment they were giving him, hopefully to learn the exercises to continue at home. It was a pointless task unless some time was given over each day to these exercises to help David's mobility.

It was at one of these sessions that concern was shown over the stiffness of David's limbs. It was suggested we saw an orthopaedic surgeon to discuss ways of surgically improving David's condition. After much discussion, it was decided that an operation be performed to release the muscles in David's groins. This would help with the general care of David and also, and more importantly, allow more movement in the hip area. At the same time, it was suggested that his hips be rotated as they were on the point of dislocating.

This would mean that David would be put in a full body plaster for six weeks, totally immobile. We were convinced it would be worthwhile in the long run, for the doctor pointed out that if David could sit better, he would not only feel better but be more socially acceptable.

He was emphatic however that in no way would this operation help David to walk. We were not expecting such a miracle anyway. David coped well with the operation which was carried out soon after. I stayed with him in hospital through the first few days and, once he was over the worst, we were able to take him home to care for him in familiar surroundings.

What we hadn't realised in bringing him home was that David was an extremely poor sleeper and, because of the possibility of pressure sores, he would need turning every two hours. This meant that as we turned him he had only just settled back into a sleep when he needed moving again.

In consequence, after only four days, I felt so tired, it seemed an impossible task to care for him 24 hours round the clock for the next five weeks, as well as keep a husband and family happy. There seemed little alternative but to have him re-admitted to hospital. Thankfully he settled in well and visiting him each day seemed the best way of spending the next few weeks.

At least I was able to have a decent night's sleep and cope with the family as well. The weeks passed quickly and in no time David was home with us again, fully recovered from his ordeal. Now, when he sat in his chair, he sat straight and his legs did not cross as they had done before. The operation seemed successful in every way.

The summer's warmth moved in to a cosy autumn and John was busy in the lounge working on a model boat. David was watching in his favourite position at the time, which was standing, with me supporting him under his armpits. We stood quietly watching what was going on. He loved to feel his feet and stood quite tall and firm-footed. "Let's go and see what daddy's doing", I said to him, expecting at this point to lift and jump him across the floor as one would a toddler learning to walk.

To my utter astonishment he stepped out one foot in front of the other and firmly walked across to see his Daddy, smiling broadly all the way. Not believing what I had just witnessed, I lifted him back to the doorway again, only for him to walk a second time, those five or six steps to the armchair where his Daddy was sitting. David was so pleased with himself, he chuckled away, whilst I just held him tight and cried tears of joy.

"I just don't believe it", I said to John and called the children to stand and watch while we tried again. Not a steady walk by any means but an intentional one, first one foot, then the other, heavy and deliberate. This was the best Christmas present I could ever have wished for. David couldn't stand unaided and definitely could not balance his own head on his shoulders evenly. Yet if he was held firmly under his armpits, with his back against my body for support, he could stride out slowly and carefully.

All at once the doctor's words came back to me. Yes, this was a miracle; it was a beginning. Determination had paid off and once again I said my prayers of thanks to God. We were overwhelmed at David's strength and awareness of his new achievement and by the end of the following summer he had attempted to walk the length of our 20 foot garden. How lovely it was to be able to go out for a walk with David in the park, then lift him from his wheelchair, for him to join in with the rest of the family.

His favourite pastime was to join in a game of football and now he could actually attempt to kick the ball himself. It was tremendous fun! Sometimes he was so full of laughter, it was difficult to keep hold of him. He chuckled so much! He was a great performer for whoever wanted to watch, and if anyone said, "Show me your new trick, David," he was always willing to oblige. He was and still is a real charmer! We were certain it was a definite attempt at walking, just as his brothers and sister had done before him, in exactly the same way. We were immensely proud of our little son and, for David, it gave a new dimension to his life.

More Surgery

1982 and, at seven years old, David stood quite tall for his age. His looks were changing, with more maturing features. Everyone marvelled at how healthy David looked and how white his new second teeth were, considering the amount of drugs he had to take. All through the bad weather, he had coped so well, travelling back and forth from school.

About this time, another great achievement had been made in as much as David had learned to use a toilet. This made life so much easier for me. I would 'potty' him in the same way as you would a baby and it really was a hit and miss affair for a short while. In fact, I had sat and looked at the adapted toilet seat for several weeks before deciding to try it out. I just felt it would be a total waste of time and effort as David was in disposable pads all the time.

It was impossible to really know whether David could make his needs known in this direction. Anyway, in no time at all, David had realised his own bodily functions and, within a few weeks, he had mastered staying dry overnight and using the toilet first thing in the morning.

David had also learned to empty his bowels each evening and for any mother who has changed nappies for a short space of time, I'm sure she'll realise my pleasure that David had achieved this feat after seven years.

However, even though he seemed well, each morning, within half an hour of waking, he would suffer a small epileptic fit, for no reason. These seemed to coincide with his early routine of toileting. The constant change of position from lying to sitting, to lying again, appeared to bring about the seizures. Armed with this information, we again visited the paediatrician. For about three months we were able to stabilize the situation with the help of increased medication but then the problem recurred.

A routine examination by an orthopaedic surgeon revealed that the left hip had in fact dislocated. X-rays were taken to confirm the fact but it was mutually decided to delay the operation for as long as was possible. Even though the fits appeared to be caused by the hip pain, we had to acknowledge it could merely be occurring because of a growth spurt; or simply ill-health because of recurrent chest infections.

However, by July of that year, the surgeon felt the operation could be delayed no longer, so it was arranged for David to be admitted during late September. To complicate matters further, David suffered a severe chest infection, so, in fact, it was November before he was fully fit enough to undergo surgery.

Feeling very nervous, we were admitted to the ward for preliminary tests and it was briefly explained that David's pelvis would be repaired by an operation called a 'Salter's osteotomy' involving some metal-work which I assumed to be a pin and plate. Everything seemed quite straight forward, so I left David to settle in for the night, returning the following morning.

David having been given a pre-medication, I went along to the operating theatre where the general anaesthetic was given. What a dreadful sinking feeling when I left the room, seeing David sleeping on that couch. I began to question myself over and over again as to whether I should have given consent for the operation and eventually satisfied myself with the thought that, had he not gone down for the operation, he would constantly be in pain and not necessarily be able to let me know just how uncomfortable he really was. I don't think it was right of me, his mother, to deny him the chance of feeling fit and healthy again and for this reason alone I had to allow the operation to be done.

It seemed an eternity waiting for him to return to the ward. I tried to eat my lunch but I was no longer hungry and the food stuck in my gullet until I thought I would choke. I attempted to read my paper but couldn't concentrate; the words held no meaning and the all-important headlines faded into obscurity. All that filled my head were thoughts of David. Please God, let him be alright.

At the end of a very long afternoon, dear David was wheeled back onto the ward. I breathed a heavy sigh of relief. The nursing staff hovered round him checking this and that and attempted to make him as comfortable as they could in the circumstances.

Once I knew he was stable and rested for the night, I also left to reassure my husband and the rest of the family and caught up on a couple of hours sleep myself. I was back on the ward again early next day and so it went on for several weeks.

David had had his hip pinned and plated in two places, so what with the after-effects of the anaesthetic, the pain of the operation and the discomfort of a full body plaster, we knew it wouldn't be plain sailing.

He stayed in hospital for three weeks but seemed to settle easier this time round and, with Christmas fast approaching, it was decided to try to manage him at home. From his prone position, he delighted in seeing the Christmas tree and decorations and in his own way joined in with all the excitement that time of year brings. It was lovely to have him home, despite the hard work and chaos it brought the rest of the family.

Christmas morning was, as usual, a very exciting and emotional time. The children were anxious to open their presents and help David to open his. There were lots of cries of laughter from everyone but quiet thoughts for me personally. It was, and still is, a time for reminiscing on what could have been. Christmas and birthdays for parents of handicapped children can be a most painful time. It can be difficult not to dwell on things for too long, for it spoils the celebrations for the rest of the family.

The youngsters really weren't into understanding my mixed feelings and I wouldn't have wanted them even to begin to think about anything other than having a wonderful day. So once again, I take a deep breath, thank God for being blessed with my little family and pray quietly that 1983 will restore David to good health.

By the end of the three weeks, David became very restless and fretful for most of the time and we returned to hospital to have the plaster removed. It was obvious then as to why. The poor little mite had some very nasty sores on his body, obviously caused as he'd gone into spasm and rubbed against the plaster caste. He'd been so brave all along and the discomfort still wasn't over. It was decided to keep David in until his skin had healed but at that time we didn't realise we were only at the beginning of another crisis.

Apparently, once the plaster had been removed, there was a problem with the healing process, for David's hip and leg began to swell and become very painful. It was very difficult to get any answers from either the nursing staff or the doctors as to why this should be happening. In fact, the medical staff in particular were extremely vague and unprofessional in their approach.

After several fraught conversations, it was decided to put David's leg in traction to ease the pressure on the hip. In theory this seemed the right course of action to take, except that David could not sit unaided, so was propped up on several pillows. He adopted a yoga position with his free leg, to help him balance. David stayed in traction for two weeks after which he was discharged. To this day, he still has a tightness in this limb.

When the great day arrived to take him home, I arrived with his wheelchair and it was only then that a severe disfigurement of the hip became apparent. Not only was the left leg a good three inches shorter than the right, the hip was set at a very strange V angle. If this had been the expected outcome of the operation, we certainly hadn't been informed.

I felt sick to the stomach as I put him in his chair to take him home, but despite everything, it was wonderful to have him home again and he seemed to be feeling the same way too. He couldn't stop laughing and smiling at everything and everybody and we realised how very much we had missed all the happiness and warmth that his company brought to our home.

Hospital outpatients appointments had been arranged but that brought us no further forward in finding out why our son was now so severely disfigured after what we had assumed to be, and had been encouraged to believe, was a routine operation. In fact, on one particular occasion the surgeon concerned in our case was quite callous in his approach. We had gone, with all good intention to discuss the situation in a logical way, but, during a brief consultation, were told the operation had gone as planned.

According to the doctor, we were being totally unreasonable in saying that David had lost his mobility. He thought the disfigurement was acceptable, that he had done exactly what he had set out to do.

So far as we were concerned, we could not understand the consequences of what we had assumed, perhaps wrongly, to be a routine operation. Those strong little legs which once took him across the living room floor and kicked purposely at a football, now flopped lifeless on the couch.

Furthermore, David could no longer sit square on a chair without extra support and his whole body adopted a windswept position. To cap it all, the toilet training he had achieved so proudly, had now stopped abruptly because David could no longer sit comfortably on his toilet seat.

Were we, was I, wrong to feel so bitter? I have since read more about cerebral palsy in young children and understood that problems do occur frequently with muscle tone and bone structure, especially with the trunk and spine, which is all due to the spasms these children suffer. How I wish this had been explained to me before, instead of leaving me to find out the hard way.

Through all this, David kept happy and smiling and I marvelled at his strength of courage and faith. He was like a ball, always willing to come bouncing back, smiling, despite everything. So, for his sake I needed to keep happy.

Since the operation, he had lost out on many activities both at home and at school. It took so long and involved too many staff to involve him in the simplest of pastimes and swimming seemed out of the question. During this time, even with his disabilities, he had learned to use his longer right leg as a sort of rudder to take him round the swimming pool like a fish. He gained confidence in the water, despite his twisted body and it was a joy to see. He was awarded a special certificate for attempting to swim the full length of the pool without giving up. All his friends at school cheered him on to that success and the framed certificate has a special place on his bedroom wall.

Anger had kept me buoyant too. I was still determined to discover what had really happened to my son. He had gone through so much in his short life it seemed so unfair. He hadn't asked to be born, least of all be born handicapped so for him to continue to suffer, in my mind, was unjustified.

For the next three years I visited a string of solicitors, took second opinions and listened to all sorts of advice but to no avail. It seems that within the medical profession, closed ranks is the order of the day if medical negligence is on the menu. There was not one doctor who felt they could assist us, despite our travelling across the country in anticipation of some support.

It would have been crucial for us to have financial aid but even that was denied us because the case appeared too difficult to prove negligence.

I felt totally dejected. It had all been a long hard fight. But worse than that, I felt I had let David down. My husband had given up sometime previously, saying that, although he could see why I wanted to fight, he couldn't envisage I could possibly win.

My children, now growing up fast into responsible teenagers were all behind my reasons to bring a case against The Health Authority. They were bitterly disappointed that it proved so complicated. So, once again, I was fighting alone to prove injustice to my son. It began to torture me and take over my life like an obsession.

The more I fought and came up against stumbling blocks, the harder I fought back. I wrote a letter to my M.P. to ask why it was the medical profession in general do not explain thoroughly and exactly what is to happen during an operation.

As a mother, I signed the operation consent form, having taken the decision for my son to be operated upon. I had trusted the doctor implicitly but to this day do not feel he had been totally honest with me. Had he explained that perhaps it wasn't possible, for whatever reason, to carry out the procedure effectively, sad though it would have been, I would have accepted the situation. But to be totally ignored and virtually 'fobbed - off' was, in my mind, unforgivable.

Had the same procedure been carried out in a normal, healthy child, there is no way it would have been accepted. However, the fact that David was already handicapped with an uncertain future, it made it all the more acceptable. After all, he was already in a wheelchair; life would be no different in that respect. The M.P. replied with every sympathy but said the case was one in which he couldn't help, because of the law as it stands.

David having a happy visit with Wendy and Ian his 'Take a Break' carers. PICTURE BY LIONEL GRECH

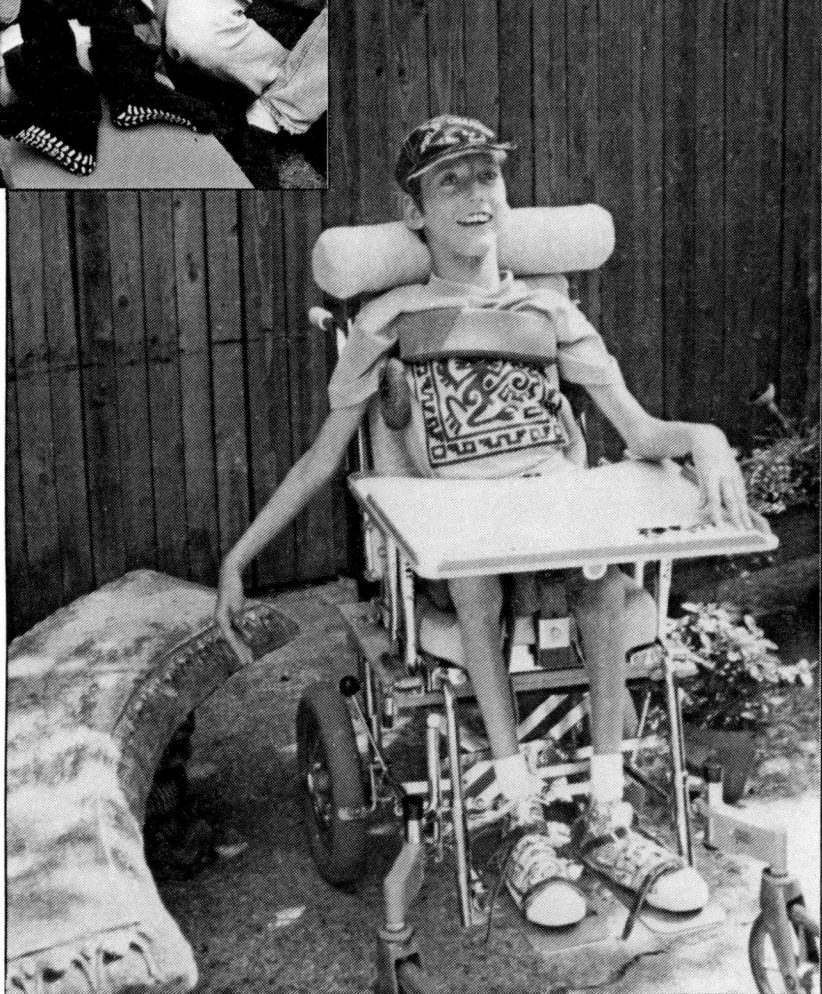

David in the garden watching birds in 1990.

David with brother Charles in a moment of contemplation.

David enjoying the garden.

David with Jenny's godson enjoying the sunshine.

David, Mum and Dad meet Yogi at Disney World.

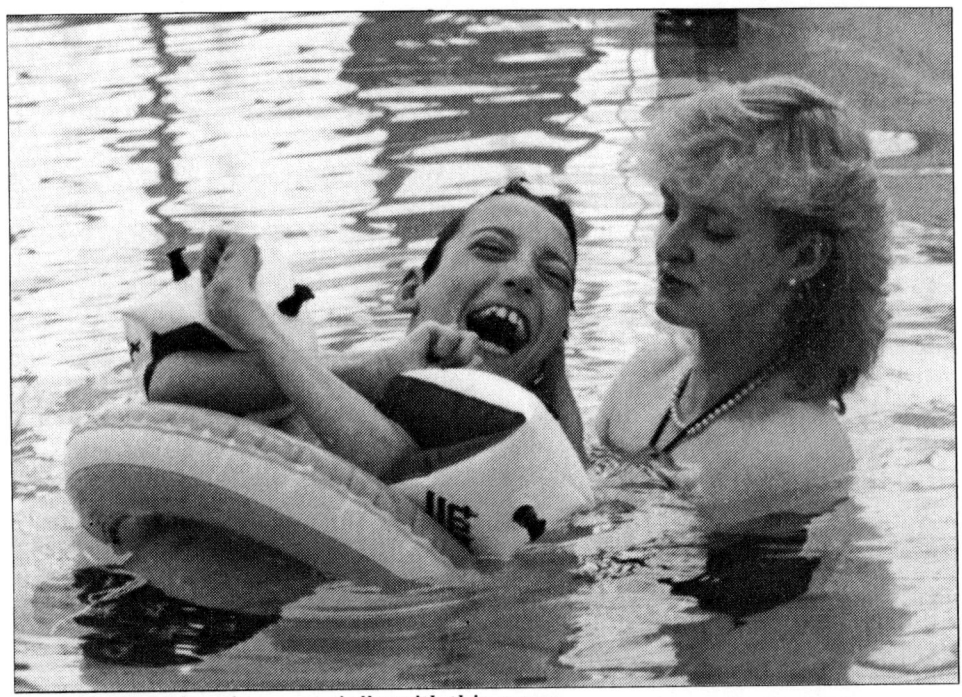

David loves swimming, especially with this carer.

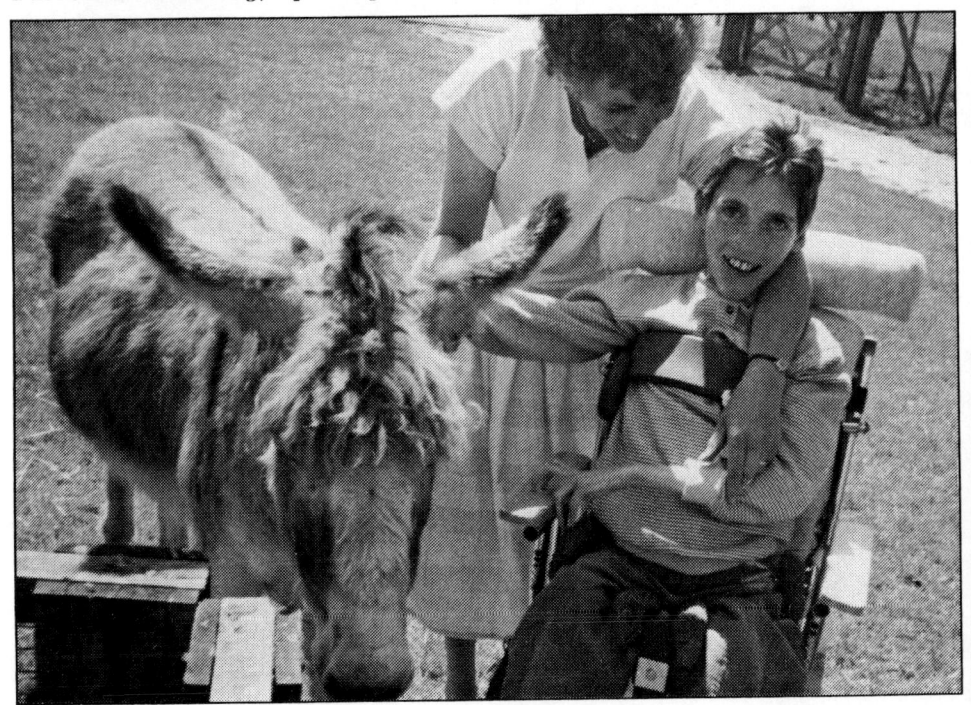

David with Mum at Whipsnade Zoo with a friendly donkey.

An Eventful Night

Despite my inner feelings of regret and sadness, there came a point in all this that I really had to stop torturing myself and stop fighting against everyone. I needed to begin again and be more logical in my approach if, ultimately, I was going to be of help to David. Feeling the way I did, there was no way I could help him, or myself.

About this time our own hospital opened and we were transferred to a new orthopaedic surgeon. The first step to improving David's discomfort was to have the pins and plates removed. This was thankfully executed without any complications. The second, and more important, step was to provide a reasonable wheelchair in which David could be comfortable. This proved far more difficult as his very windswept posture did not allow for him to sit square in anything that was readily available and the spasms had affected his legs drastically.

After a lot of to-ing and fro-ing without success, it was suggested that the problem be tackled with the use of medication. This certainly seemed the best solution, especially if it would help David sit more comfortably. An appointment was made to see a specialist at another hospital nearby.

The doctors explained the procedure thoroughly and we were told the drug used to stop the spasm in his trunk and limbs would be administered directly into his lower spine. Obviously David would be kept in hospital for observation afterwards. Agreeing that we should at least try this treatment, with bags packed, I travelled with David to the hospital. I asked to sleep off the ward as David was never a good sleeper at the best of times and, should he wake in the night and see me, there would be no rest for either of us.

The treatment appeared very straightforward. David was to have the pre-med followed by a lumbar puncture to administer the drug. This, in turn, would relax his hips and legs, allowing him once again to sit square and comfortable in his wheelchair. I should have known better! When did anything ever go smoothly in our life?

David had the pre-med and was sound asleep within minutes. He was then taken to the treatment room and returned to the ward shortly afterwards. Whilst he slept, I had my tea and then went for a soak in the bath. On my return David was still sleeping, so I thought I'd have half an hour in front of the television to catch up on the news of the day.

By ten o'clock we were making our own headline news! I had come back into the ward to find David in a coma. He was barely breathing, his pulse and blood pressure had dropped dramatically and his body temperature had fallen to 32.3 degrees. Within seconds of finding him in this state, he was wrapped in a survival blanket and whisked into a side-ward that had glaring hot wall heaters. Whilst I stood totally rooted to the spot at David's bedside, sweating profusely with the intense heat, the medical team gave David counter-reacting drugs and worked the whole night through to bring his body temperature up to normal.

It was 6.30 in the morning before David was out of danger. I have never, ever, been so frightened or prayed so much in all my life. Once again, I thought, why me? What have I done to deserve all this? Then I thought: selfish, selfish, me. The worry is to my son, what has he done to endure so much pain and suffering? I had, yet again, thought I was doing the best for David, by allowing this treatment.

I began to question whether I should have agreed to David having more drugs, more treatment. I was only trying to improve his quality of life. I thought it was the right decision. I asked David and God for forgiveness. I had only done what I felt was right for my child.

There seemed little point in calling John at such an early hour, so I rang later that morning. There was little he could have done anyway and I was just so thankful I could tell him all was well again. People passing in the corridor must have thought I was quite loony, laughing and crying at the same time. The total relief I felt that David was still alive after such a trauma was overwhelming. It was later described by the ward staff as being quite an eventful night but inexplicable why David had reacted the way he had.

Following that setback, it was obvious we had to find an alternative solution to David's seating and posture problems. Thankfully, some months later, we were referred to The Chailey Heritage, a seating clinic and residential home for children with special needs in Sussex. This was to hold the answer to all our dreams and fears. We were advised that a further operation would be essential to allow David to sit normally again. His tiny body, only weighing three and half stone, had become so disfigured and twisted over the years, there was no way a seat could be of help at this late stage.

The operation, as it was explained to us both, sounded very drastic indeed but apparently had been very successful on other children suffering from the same problem. It entailed removing the ball joint of each hip, and possibly up to four inches of his femur, in order to remove all the disfigurement on the left side of his thigh. The same procedure would have to be carried out at the same time on the right side, in order for the legs and hips to be made even. David would have to be in bed for 6-8 weeks with both legs on traction, whilst the hips healed and the remaining bones in the upper thighs found their own level.

We were worried whether this should be attempted at all but then, what were the alternatives? Already David had begun to have digestive problems because he was so twisted. Things were not going to improve, only get worse in fact, and I, for one, couldn't begin to see David in such discomfort.

Together my husband and I discussed the situation. In the past it had been I who had signed the consent form, in my mind taking full responsibility for David's welfare. That burden had weighed heavily over the years and this time I wasn't prepared to go it alone.

Both John and I decided we wanted to go ahead with the operation but we also needed to discuss it fully with the family and all those that knew and cared for David. We weren't asking for justification but we were trying to explain the logic behind our decision.

It seemed the only option open to us to give David a chance for enjoying whatever life he had left. We hoped they would understand our reasons and thankfully they did. For a while, life returned to normal whilst we waited for an admission date.

Sad News At Christmas

There has never been any question of David being anyone other than a brother to the rest of the family. Even though they have different fathers, David is their brother, none of this step-brother situation. They have grown incredibly close over the years. Nicholas or Nik as he now prefers to be called, once remarked that everyone should have a disabled child in his home for a month, just for the experience. Then, he said, people would begin to understand and not call awful names and jibes. He was about eight years old at the time, going on twenty-five!

John and I have always tried to be good, understanding parents to the children, despite all the traumas which have occurred, and continue to occur, in their short lives. Their own father moved away when we made our move but, over the years, still kept in touch and saw them as often as was possible. He was rebuilding his life too, whilst we tried to do the same; and he would visit or have the children to stay with him. Naturally, there were times when the children resented John taking control of their lives at home and we tried to work through this together.

It wasn't always plain-sailing and there were always problems of some sort but I'm thankful now for the time they had to share with their father. They all enjoyed nothing more than a relaxing time with him. I was, I suppose, quite a strict mother, hopefully loving and kind but very disciplined. Max was far more free and easy and for the family to stay with him and not have such restrictions was, I'm sure, total bliss. It was here they could come and go as they pleased, stay up late, watch as much T.V. as they could, whilst eating their meal between two slices of bread. There was no sitting at a laid table, using knife and fork, having to remember table manners.

Jayne was his little girl in whom he never ceased to marvel and yet, at the same time, he constantly worried how she would fair in this changing, difficult world. The boys were his pride and joy and he always hoped they would develop his keen sense of fun, have the ability to stand by what they believed in but maintain their sensitivity and charm.

In one sense, John became the children's security and a father figure whilst Max became a cherished friend and Dad like no other could. We maintained a good friendship after the initial difficulties of our divorce and he was constantly supportive of John, David and myself, showing endless sympathy and understanding.

It was, then, a tremendous shock to learn that he had suffered severe head injuries in a freak accident a couple of weeks before Christmas 1987. Sadly, he died on 18th December and we buried him on Christmas Eve. We stood alongside his own children, dear mother, brother and wife, all united in the same grief.

This must have been the saddest time of our children's lives and, for myself and John, Christmas will never be the same again. As I have already said earlier, we were always very proud of our children. They had not been outstanding scholars, achieving great academic heights but they have never failed to be good, honest and loving people with a special perception of the value of life. I believe this had been enhanced by having David in the family and by experiencing the loss of people dear to them.

As they have grown and matured, I can see the same special qualities in my sons and daughter as I recognised in their father and it brings me great comfort. My daughter Jayne, now married herself to a very caring and loving young man, misses her own father very deeply and Timothy, her husband, has been a great strength to her and to us all. Jayne was always her Daddy's little girl and, in my heart, I know he looks down on her and her brothers with the same warmth and love he would give if he were still with us. He would have been proud of them.

We now no longer take things for granted. Our lives have been touched and enriched by loving and losing and each is a precious memory.

The Loss Of A Friend

It was in June 1988 that David was admitted to hospital again for the operation on his hips. At the time, I was really very worried, for his health seemed so poor and I knew we were taking a great risk in allowing this operation. Yet, if it weren't performed, his life expectancy could be reduced anyway, so I prayed to God that we had made the right decision.

Once again, I accompanied David to the operating theatre, holding his little hand as we passed down the corridors. I left him in the capable hands of the surgeon and the nursing staff and retreated to the parents' room to down eternal cups of tea during the long wait. It was four hours before he was returned to the ward on his hospital bed, which looked very forbidding with the overhead traction coming down to support his tiny bandaged legs.

I stood at the side of his bed feeling intensely scared and frightened for his safe return to good health and, in no time at all, his doctors came on to the ward to check David and to assure me that everything was all right. So different from all previous experiences with surgeons! Here was David's surgeon, totally and utterly concerned for David's welfare and our peace of mind. He sat down alongside us and explained every detail of the operation. He didn't pull any punches, either. It would not be an easy pathway back to good health. Apart from the slow healing process of the extensive scars, because David would be lying on his back for, at a minimum, 6 weeks, it was inevitable that pneumonia could occur at any time. There was also a danger of infection because of the incontinence problems, which couldn't be avoided and physiotherapy had to be started immediately to ease his chest problems. The bed was also tipped back to help drain his chest, so feeding in this position might be a problem and, lastly, bed-sores would be a certainty. The doctor comforted us and assured us that whatever was needed would be done, so we felt quite reassured with his concern.

However, David, being David, as always, surprised us all. Within just a few hours of the operation, he was awake and responding. Constant painkilling injections were needed to keep him calm and pain free. Drinking proved to be a little difficult but nothing that couldn't be overcome with feeding cups. In fact, he developed a healthy appetite, despite the unnatural position in which he was lying.

I stayed with David for the first two nights after the operation. He needed me there and I wanted to be there. John was working nights so would come in to see us before he started work and on his return in the morning.

It was on the third morning that, after he had come in to see us, he returned shortly after with the tragic news of Pauline's death. She had died on 19th June 1988, from a severe asthma attack. It was her youngest son's birthday and Father's Day. I was devastated, for I had only spoken to her the previous evening to reassure her that David was all right after his operation. She worried so much about him. The sadness I feel in the loss of my dearest friend cannot be put into words. Because she was so special to me, to my family, and especially to David - she loved him as her own - it is important to us that she is remembered in this book.

Life came to a standstill that day. The nursing staff were very sympathetic. I needed to go home and be with John and the children. I explained to David why I had to leave him for a while and that he was in good hands whilst I was away. I didn't think I'd be of any help to anyone if I stayed on the ward. I'd lost my best friend, my sister. My heart ached.

On my return the following day, I needn't have worried. David had had several visitors to keep him happy. I tried to put David's needs first again. It was very difficult to concentrate my mind but it worked. I certainly needed something to take my thoughts off my grief and keep me cheerful. Thankfully, as always, David was my saviour and it was he who made me smile again.

The weather was glorious throughout June and July and we managed occasionally to wheel David out into the hospital grounds, traction intact, into the sunshine. He always looked much better with some sun to his face; it brought out his freckles by the hundred. And so we managed to face another day; and another week.

He was so cheerful, always full of smiles, despite the pain and discomfort he must have been in. After nearly five weeks in hospital, it was decided he could come home for the final few weeks. We would have all the back-up services which could be provided and so it seemed the right decision to make. It was just that getting him home proved difficult. He needed to be transported on his bed but there were no ambulances available to do this. It would be difficult to strip down an ambulance, so we had to re-think the situation.

Neighbours of ours who have a removal service came to our rescue. We waited until their working day was over and then prepared David for the short but difficult journey home. The traction was taken off the bed and put to one side; then David's legs were bound tightly together, so as to immobilise him.

The removal van parked outside the main entrance to the hospital and we said our goodbyes to the ward staff and began to wheel David on his bed down the corridors and out of the building. How I wished I'd got a video camera at that moment! Everyone stood about watching the proceedings: staff who had come outside to say 'Cheerio' and visitors who were just leaving the hospital. We certainly drew the crowds.

It took six people to push David's bed sideways up the ramp of the van. He disappeared inside with cheers all round and thought the whole event so funny, he wouldn't stop laughing.

Once parked outside the house after the short journey from the hospital, we again gave the neighbours something to smile about. The nurse and I began to carry this child heavily wrapped from head to foot like an Egyptian mummy, out of the van and into the house. The bed wouldn't go through the front door and through our hall, so it had to be dismantled and taken round the side of the house. Fortunately, David's bedroom is downstairs and has french windows, so at least that was made easier. After about another hour, we had managed between us to get David's traction set up and made him comfortable for the night.

He seemed so pleased to be back home with all his own toys and family round him again. It had been a long hard five weeks. But we weren't out of the woods yet.

Whilst David was in traction and his head in a tipped position, he seemed to progress really well but, once the traction was removed and he was able to lie freely in his bed, the discomfort returned with a vengeance, together with a lack of appetite.

I wasn't sure whether he was making some stand as to how much he had suffered over the past two months but he virtually went on a starvation diet. We had to resort to using nourishing build-up type drinks in an effort to keep his weight up but we were getting nowhere fast.

Coupled with the loss of weight, David began to get more pain in his hips, so it was mutually decided to re-admit him to hospital for a short while. He was treated with antibiotics and put on a light traction to relieve the pressure in his thighs. His hips eventually healed but he required constant intense physiotherapy to bring some movement into these very floppy legs.

I can recall, whilst he was still in hospital, asking the orthopaedic surgeon if I could see the X-rays of his hips. I had to try to come to terms with David's new bone structure. He had lost several inches of his upper thighs and felt very loose and floppy round the hip area. In time, we were told, the muscle tone would increase, and some movement would return. In the meantime I needed to nurse David, change and lift him around, so I had to re-educate myself to his new physical state.

Seeing the X-rays was quite shocking mentally and it took some days to get it into my head how his little body was now. Like a 'bendy' toy is a simple description. His legs would move into any direction that I wanted. In effect, this greatly helped when the time came to get his new wheelchair fitted. It was just such a pity it had to be done so quickly in September, almost immediately after he had come off the traction. He didn't like being moved very much and certainly having to sit upright and at a 90 degree angle was extremely uncomfortable for him.

The staff at the unit in Sussex were very helpful and sympathetic and, with their workmanship and expertise, we came away with the best fitting wheelchair David had ever been able to sit in.

Two and a half years later, as I write this, he is still able to use it and hopefully it should be comfortable for some time yet. Returning from Sussex with this new wheelchair, it seemed we could begin to face a happier future, with David sitting more naturally, free from further orthopaedic problems.

My daughter, Jayne, and her fiance had planned to marry on 29th October 1988, so we had lots of organising to do in between caring for our son. It was to be a church wedding with 120 guests, five bridesmaids and all the principal men in formal dress. I made Jayne's three tier wedding cake in some snatched spare moments, then it was handed over to a close friend to do the honours with the icing and decoration. Planning the day with all the trimmings to give our only daughter a wonderful send-off was the tonic we needed in darker moments when our spirits sank to the depths of despair.

With the wedding of the year to look forward to, we had hoped that David could share the day with us. Unfortunately he had returned to the hospital suffering a further chest infection. John felt very privileged to give this young bride away to the man she loved, and she really looked beautiful. Her grandmother made a very touching speech on behalf of Max bringing tears to everyone's eyes. The wedding day was also James's 18th birthday and how we all wished their Dad could have been there to share such a special day. He certainly wasn't far from our thoughts, and neither was Pauline. Thankfully the day went off without a hitch and everyone had a lovely time. The sun shone and, for a short while, we were able to indulge ourselves without looking over our shoulder.

Because of continuing bad health following the operation, it took David some time to recover fully. In fact, it would be difficult to say just how many times we returned to hospital within the eighteen months of the surgery. The operation and the effects which must have taken its toll on his little body but David, being the fighter he is, continued to battle back despite several bouts of bronchitis and pneumonia.

Although David started back to school in September 1988, it wasn't to last and, after twelve months of very spasmodic attendance, it was decided to send him on a part-time basis. He had lost out on all his school outings, which he enjoyed so much, as well as the Christmas celebrations and annual school holidays. All were shelved or cancelled completely because he was just not able to enjoy them whilst in such bad health. After a full week at school, he would come home looking so tired and spend most of the weekend sleeping from sheer exhaustion.

David so enjoyed school and put such energy and enthusiasm into every day, it was a pity to see him not well enough to cope. He was still very good at applying himself to using the computer with the special touch pad. All the cause and effect machines he could use with ease and school assemblies and social occasions would be the highlight of the week. Still, this was not doing him any good if he was weakening and, with little resistance, it was only making him ill again. He was wide open to any infection he came into contact with, especially in school.

The last time he went into hospital, in March 1989, was the turning point. He had been so poorly, even antibiotics didn't seem to provide their miraculous cure as in the past.

On one of my visits, when David was so poorly that his health was causing anxieties to us all, the sister took me aside for a cup of tea and an honest, forthright talk. She explained how they had tried their best for David, pulling him through at every crisis but perhaps he was saying in his own way that he wanted to be left alone.

It was decided that I take him home and give him all the love and cuddles he needed at this time. No more medical intervention other than his normal daily medication.

We cried together and she was so caring for us all as a family; it must have been painful for her too. We had built up a friendship over the years and, now the barriers were down, uniforms and status put aside, there was just simple caring and love. David had become their friend too and they were also sad that things weren't going to get any better.

I knew in my heart that David was really poorly now but I had also had a gut feeling from the first day of his diagnosis that he would only live into his early teens. At this time, he was approaching his fourteenth birthday and it was almost as though I had been prepared for this to happen. Yet it was difficult to comprehend life without David - it didn't seem like it could be possible; David should be with us always.

I couldn't bring myself to say anything to the other children that day, nor to dear John either. I went home and slept on my grief for another twenty four hours. David's

Dad had found it so difficult at the beginning to accept the fact that his child was not perfect. He had married me, a divorcee with four young children, whom, yes, he loved and cared for and he had made a good parent. But those children were not his own flesh and blood. All his hopes and dreams for his son had been shattered the day cerebral palsy was diagnosed and, whilst he had an intense love for David, he had never truly accepted the situation for real.

It is apparently quite normal for fathers to feel this way, which means the care and worry is often put on the mother. The emotional worry has always reached my heart but often sunk to my boots at times. With John, his emotional feelings for David sit on the perimeter of his heart, because, if the reality of it tries to sink in, it would break. He has to be the breadwinner, the provider and an excellent caring job he has made of that. He loves me to bits and I know it, as do the children. However, ask him to give David an enema, change a dirty nappy or sit up and nurse David every night for a week and he wouldn't cope alone.

Over the years I've learned to accept the situation, though it's not been an easy one, far from it. Sometimes I've found our life really hard to cope with but, at the end of the day, I've had to reflect back to what made me love John in the very beginning. When I do, all those feelings come rushing back and I can't say anything to him but that I love him with all my heart. Someday, when all the family have grown up and flown the nest and David is no longer with us, I would hope that John and I could really enjoy each others company again, as we did all those years ago.

So, the following day, when I brought David home and John and I were sitting quietly with him, I explained as sensitively as I could, exactly what the nurse had told me.

As I expected, John was totally shattered and for some minutes he was speechless. We cried together, as we had done fourteen years ago and shared our grief, holding on tight to each other.

We thought how, if we had the money, we could take David to Disney World, with all its colour and excitement. He would love that! However, we were broke, as always but felt we needed to go away on our own with David for a short break. It would help us to come to terms with the future and give us the strength to tell the rest of the family and all those who have known David what the situation was.

We rang around the holiday camps and found a self-catering chalet available on the east coast; so we booked a long weekend. It was lovely to get away and the weather was good to us.

We spent a lot of time on our own after David had gone to bed, talking through the situation and we decided it would be for the best to go home and try to carry on life as normally as possible. We would prepare the children but at no time did we want the inevitable to rule our lives. We needed to enjoy whatever time we had left with David and the rest of the family and leave it all in God's hands.

The break was really lovely and David enjoyed all the car rides and walks by the sea. By the time we returned, we all looked and felt better for the break.

Just as we expected, the family were totally numbed by the news but then, as we said, David was still with us, so we just had to get on with life and enjoy his company and try not to get too depressed. This was really hard to begin with, as each time David was poorly, we all panicked and thought the worst. Slowly, his general health began to pick up again and, by September, he was able to enjoy a caravan holiday with John and me by the sea. It was wonderful to see him looking well and enjoying life, continually laughing and in good spirits.

He returned to school in September 1989 and was able to go swimming for the first time in ages. This did wonders to tone up his little muscles and it was good to see him enjoying the experience of the hydrotherapy pool. Soon he was beginning to move his legs himself and, at long last, we felt he was improving.

The Will To Go On Living

One thing David never lost during all his health problems was his wonderful warmth and sense of humour. Once he was over the worst, his infectious laugh was there again and he was ready to share a joke or funny experience. He was still incredibly nosy about everything that was going on around him. He never did like missing out on anything.

The weeks and months passed and he got stronger by the minute, once more amazing us all and the medical profession by his strength of character. The scars had all healed very well and the resulting effect made the operation and everything worthwhile.

By Christmas 1989 he seemed to reach the peak of good health, though sadly, the right leg, which had caused problems before the final operation, still seemed to be a worry because it continued to be uncomfortable whatever position he sat in. Nevertheless, we could always sit David in his wheelchair without discomfort. We needed to keep his legs extra warm as he was quite immobile, so we used lots of warm socks and blankets to help his circulation. For the first time in ages David was able to enjoy Christmas and all the happy events going on around him. We had a wonderful time opening gifts for him and he was enthralled by the excitement of it all.

He laughed his way through Christmas and the happiness he felt reflected through us all. We had managed to bring ourselves safely through yet another year.

1990, and time to make New Year resolutions. I had decided to start the year with a very positive attitude. When the nurse had spoken to me the previous March, she had said it could be a matter of weeks or months before David died or possibly not for some time yet; only he could decide when enough was enough.

There were times through the past months when I had sat up with him all night, cuddling the tired little frame of my beloved son, almost feeling my own palms against my chest, he was so weak and empty. I had on many occasions told him not to hang on, should he want to quietly slip away, he had that control. I am his mother, not his keeper. I would tell him 'If you've had enough David, don't stay on in this life just for me or anyone else. It's your choice and you must go when you've had enough. Besides, there are others who loved you, just waiting on the world beyond to take care of you.'

But David, being David, fought back again and again and here we are just starting yet another New Year and he's approaching his sixteenth birthday. He's looking very frail as usual and sometimes quite drawn with mauve rings around his eyes but those eyes are still bright and shining as always with that mischievous twinkle glinting there. With summer approaching and a few freckles on his cheeks, it will improve his youthful good looks without doubt. Those bright blue eyes are just as appealing and his smile and laughter as touching and infectious, despite constant chest problems and painful limbs. My guess is, being the stubborn little lad that he is, he'll continue in this same way until he's good and ready to leave.

Life for David has always been limited, as we so called 'normal' people know it- but for David it's none the less enjoyable and too good to miss. In his life, he has had so many problems to cope with and I just hope, as a parent, I've not been too thoughtless and harsh on him. The decisions I had to make were for his benefit in the long run to enable David to live as full a life as was possible.

When David suffered, I, as his mother, suffered with him and his family alongside us both. All I ever wanted was the best for David and I hope he'll not think I've put him through unnecessary pain and suffering to achieve this. Wherever David has gone, whoever David has met, no-one has ever failed to be touched by the happy and loving child that he is.

The greatest pleasure in looking after David throughout these sixteen years has been the excitement of witnessing all his achievements. Not just the ability he gained to walk but all the little things one takes for granted in a normal child. The laughs, chuckles and warmth when he recognises people dear to him. The apprehension of a strange face or an unfamiliar place. The love of company and the sadness if he is left alone, perhaps in different surroundings. The joy he gains from being with his brothers, sister and ever extending family and their complete acceptance of him as one of them.

Through going to school, he has learned to travel well, loved seeing new places with friends. He has accepted that other people are there to help him be comfortable, change his pads and dress him up again; feed him his meals and offer him his favourite cup of tea. He can demolish a large soft ice-cream cone just as quick as his Dad now, and relishes every mouthful.

He loves animals. We have a dog, Brandy, and two cats; Claws and Alfie, who all show great affection for this young lad that allows them to cuddle up close.

David has learned many new skills with the limited use of his right hand. He uses most of the specialist toys in his department at school with ease and loves sharing the laughter that continually surrounds school life.

We moved from our first home in this area to a more suitable house, where we were able to have special adaptations carried out to help David live in comfort. We chose a blue theme in his rooms, with brightly coloured curtains with rainbow patterns. He feels comfortable there and enjoys being put to bed, to listen to a favourite tape whilst he falls asleep, surrounded by his favourite soft toys and reading books.

On a bad day when we can't get out for our usual walk round the village, he loves to watch his football videos and really enters into the spirit of the game, with shrieks and laughs as the goals are scored or missed. With three older brothers who have been brought up with football, there's no wonder, I suppose, that David should have the same enthusiasm. Even though he's not as able in water as he used to be, he still loves swimming and that trip to the pool each week with school friends is a treat he loves.

A Life Worth Living

Through all the traumas and the tears, it has been a joy and a privilege, to care for David. He has enriched our lives and those that have known him. He has filled our hearts with a love and happiness that is quite indescribable and every memory is dearly cherished.

When a couple have a baby, they love and care for that child and want only the best that life can offer him. They accept every stage in his development as normal, not thinking for one moment it could be any different. But if you give birth to a child with any degree of handicap, life is really never the same again. Every step in that child's development is a miracle in itself but you have to fight every step of the way. It is so important to keep it all in perspective.

People have said, in their naivete, such things as, "At least you have other children". Believe me, it is no consolation but it does make you more appreciative of your healthy family and I frequently count my blessings. With David, the first smile, the recognition of a familiar face, the outstretched fingers, feeling and exploring- it's like magic. The sheer warmth of the cuddles at the end of the day is wonderful.

Holidays, too are all happy memories. Before we moved here, we spent two holidays on the South Coast with all the children in a rented bungalow about half-a-mile from the sea. We also had the added luxury of a good sized beach hut which, with the bad weather we experienced, was great to be able to use. The older children loved to go down to the beach, rain or shine to play at the waters edge and have sandcastle competitions amongst themselves.

We have fond memories of rainy days and ice-creamed faces, playing ball games on the promenade or kite-flying escapades. The little stove in the beach hut was just the job to prepare warm drinks and mugs of soup when we returned from a long walk along the beach, totally deserted except for the trail of little footsteps and wheelprints in the damp sand for the tide to take away.

With David growing fast, travelling became a problem with five young children, a wheelchair, toys, picnic basket and everything, it seemed, but the kitchen sink. Even the shortest journey needed careful planning. It was decided to exchange our saloon car for an old green Bedford van. This proved to be the best car sale we ever made.

The van was just a shell inside and John set about fitting it out with side bench seats and a secure place for David to sit in his specially adapted travel chair. Windows were installed so the children had a view as we travelled and, finally, it was kitted out with a portable stove, china and kitchen utensils.

The times spent on holiday with this van must be amongst our happiest times together.

One year, we travelled to North Wales on a sight-seeing holiday. We borrowed a large tent in which we slept and used our van as a kitchen/diner. On the first night, I was concerned how well David would take to sleeping in a sleeping bag on the ground. I needn't have worried for he went off like a top.

The following morning he had us and our children, in fits of laughter. As I brought him out in his wheelchair to feed him his breakfast, he kept looking at me and then up at the sky and all around. I think he finally thought I'd flipped my lid, eating outside at such an early hour. He just laughed and laughed until we thought he'd burst.

He didn't eat much breakfast that morning with all the excitement.

That old van enabled us to travel round and enjoy our holidays together or even just the odd few days during school breaks. It was important that the older children would still enjoy themselves; even with everything that had to be done for David, we could still be a normal family unit.

As David got older and needed even more attention, it became difficult to spend time away as a complete family. As much as we enjoyed ourselves, because of David's health problems, he required constant attention. So holidays were no longer a time for rest; it was just that everything was done in different surroundings. Also, with the other children growing fast, there were always things we wanted to do just with them.

The rest of the family were always more than understanding of David's needs but even the simplest of trips became increasingly difficult. Whilst on holiday, we might want to climb a steep hill or go to the top of a windmill to admire the view but, with the wheelchair, it often meant David would be left out or we would have to go out at separate times, because it wasn't suitable to take David along. It seemed the family's life was becoming more limited and it needed careful re-thinking to keep the balance.

It was about this time that a new residential care home opened in our district. David would be eligible to go for short-term breaks, long weekends and occasional nights and in turn it meant we could go out and about with his brothers and sister.

Once everyone accepted the idea in the full knowledge that David was being well cared for with his friends and extended family at the home, we were able to look forward to the times when we could totally relax and enjoy ourselves. It was a small home, beautifully designed and only seven children on each overnight stay, so it was very much a warm, friendly and loving environment.

This care has continued over the years and whilst, in the beginning, it was a wrench to give David's care over to other people, in my heart, I knew I was making a positive step towards David's independence. To allow him to go from me was not just to ease the strain but to allow him to grow as a young boy and give him a social life outside the confines of home that he might not otherwise experience.

With this decision, I was giving David interests away from the family he knew and, hopefully, he would also learn to love and appreciate these new friends.

More recently he has been 'adopted' by a young couple who do not have any children of their own. This is a scheme run by the local Social Services Department. They are able to care for him as we require, usually up to a 36 hour break once a month or so. This is just enough time to have a good night's rest and re-charge the batteries. The couple care for him and love him as their own and so, with these two support systems, the strain of caring for David, now severely handicapped, is greatly eased.

I am sure life has been made more enjoyable because of the patience and understanding of my older children. Unfortunately, because of the constant demands caring for David has put on my time, the others had to learn tolerance and independence at an early age. Somehow, they have managed to survive and emerged as warm, friendly and interesting young adults. It could not have been easy for them growing up, not knowing from day to day how life would turn out. Often our best laid plans would have to be shelved because of David's ill-health.

They took it all in their stride, with little or no complaint. Since leaving school and entering into the working world, they have been able to respond to both John and me on equal ground and now get along very well together. They, in turn, have developed great respect and love for John, for they realise now, being adults themselves, how hard he has worked to support this family which he took on because of his love for me, their mother.

Being head of the household was not an enviable position for John to be in. Despite obvious affection, there were often jealousies and confrontations and not being their natural father had its problems. He has always enjoyed D.I.Y. and car mechanics, yet none of the children shared his ability. On the other hand, he would duck out of any form of leisurely healthy excercise which in turn would irritate them.

Still, as a family, we have tried over the years to talk through our worries and problems and in so doing, we hope we've avoided at least some of the bad feeling and resentment caused by arguments between teenagers and parents.

John continues to work very long shifts and the children are aware of the commitment he has to his role of husband and provider, and respect him for his steadfastness, when life has been so difficult.

Over the years, Jayne has worked hard to become a very successful secretary although her one big ambition is to become a mother one day. I hope and pray she will be fulfilled.

It certainly seems strange to see James following in his own father's footsteps, working for the health authority but he is well-suited to the compassionate role he plays within the hospital. And Nik, who married Suzanne recently, has a responsible position with a large communications company, as does Charles, too.

No-one could ever replace Max; he was and still is very special to all the children. Yet John has at least helped to fill the void that was left when their father died. Over the years, he has come to love them all very deeply, as his own, and together we are immensely proud of them, as Max would be too.

The pressures of bringing up such a large family, with the added problems with David, have now eased and we can look back and smile, remembering the good times and the bad with great affection. I have been very fortunate to continue with part-time jobs and community work since David's health has greatly improved and it has given me something else to focus my life on now that the family are flying the nest.

Reflecting on all David's problems, I thank God he has managed to overcome them and gone on to enjoy his life within its limitations. We are so thankful he continues to love life.

My biggest wish, that John and I could come together again instead of being like ships that pass in the night, has also been granted. Amidst all this, we have managed to maintain our sanity, humour and love for one another and actually have managed a couple of holidays on our own, which were wonderful.

If I have any regret, it is that the so-called qualified doctors and medical staff were not as honest or sympathetic at times as they could have been. Maybe more explanations and truthful talking would have helped along the way when caring for David and, certainly, compassion early on in his life might have eased the pain for all of us. Yet, given a second chance, I don't think I'd want to change things, for the experience of caring for my son has enhanced our lives beyond compare.

O.K. There are drawbacks, I suppose, in caring for someone like David. We cannot just go off, without first considering who is caring for David in our absence and, if I analysed our lot, it would be depressing. But, we've come this far and still managed somehow and I'm not one for feeling depressed for long. Life is for living and enjoying whatever the limitations. Today's a lovely day, the sun is shining and we'll get through. Tomorrow, who knows? We'll face that when it comes.

As David's mother, I feel so privileged to have been given the chance to share his life. I know his father, family and friends feel enriched by the experience too. He has always been the rainbow in my life, there ready with a smile and a laugh on a bad day. When David eventually does take the final journey to heaven, I know life will be difficult and bereft without him. Yet I also know I will have so many happy memories to bring out the rainbow on those rainy days.

Epilogue

It is now some time since I finished writing this book and I am delighted that it has been published. I hope it will be of some comfort and encouragement for other families who have found themselves in similar circumstances to mine.

I have never ceased to wonder at David's resilience and can hardly believe that this year he will reach his eighteenth birthday. He has fought back so many times from life threatening illnesses and is at present amazing us all by his enjoyment of life at home and at school.

David is well able to make his needs known by sounds, facial expressions and a strong eye-to-eye contact and is beginning to use a communications board and digitalised speech machine, operated by a touch pad. Whilst these skills are all at a very elementary stage, it is still tremendously exciting for both us his family and David himself who expresses great pleasure in being able to be understood.

Life, as always, has been busy caring for my son on a daily basis and juggling everything else around his ever-demanding routine.

We've had more happy holidays and the family is ever-increasing with both the weddings of Nik to Suzanne and James to Laura in the past couple of years. Home life has takeen on a new dimension with the family gathering for Sunday lunch or evening coffee when we sit up and catch up on the news of the day and it goes without saying that the children are always a constant source of happiness and support to John and I.

David continues to have more frequent bouts of ill-health due to recurrent chest problems and, because of his increasing immobility, this has meant I have had to incorporate a routine of chest and body physiotherapy into his daily care programme. Antibiotics have long since become ineffective, with his immune system failing gradually and he also suffers occasional sickness for no apparent reason. However, providing all those people who deal with David on a day-to-day basis continue to be supportive, between us we manage to give him a good quality of life despite his ever-frail body, weighing now just two and a half stones.

Whilst David is in good health, he is always bright, alert, responsive and smiling; we value and appreciate these times for we continue to live with the knowledge that we could lose our son tomorrow. That part doesn't get any easier with the passing of time.

I wrote this poem late into the night when David was poorly some years ago but I think it sums up still my feelings for my very special son.

For David

Take his hand, set him free.
Guide him happily away from me.
Help him walk, let him run.
All those things he couldn't have done.
Let him jump, see the fun,
Ride a bike, kick a ball,
Not toe the line - do it all!
Read a book, tell a joke,
Love conversation with other folk.
Smile completely, no more pain.
Free as a bird. Brave and strong,
Go fly over that rainbow, David,
Till we meet again.

On 20th August 1994 whilst on holiday, David decided it was the right time to fly over the rainbow. This book now seems a fitting memory for a little boy who was so special to so many. I hope you think so too.